EXPLORE YOUR WORLD

By Jeffrey B Fuerst

Series Literacy Consultant
Dr Ros Fisher

Pearson Education Limited
Edinburgh Gate
Harlow
Essex CM20 2JE
England

www.longman.co.uk

ISBN 0 582 84143 7

Colour reproduction by Colourscan, Singapore
Printed and bound in China by Leo Paper Products Ltd.

The Publisher's policy is to use paper manufactured from sustainable forests.

10 9 8 7 6 5 4 3 2

The following people from **DK** have
contributed to the development of this product:

Art Director Rachael Foster

Martin Wilson **Managing Art Editor**	**Managing Editor** Marie Greenwood
Spencer Holbrook **Design**	**Editorial** Julie Ferris
Brenda Clynch **Picture Research**	**Production** Gordana Simakovic
Richard Czapnik, Andy Smith **Cover Design**	**DTP** David McDonald

Consultant Roger Few

Dorling Kindersley would like to thank: Andy Crawford for photography and Peter Bull for original artwork. Rose Horridge,
Gemma Woodward, and Hayley Smith in the DK Picture Library. Johnny Pau for additional cover design work. Lily Dang, Rohan Francis,
and Sasha Watson for modelling work.

Picture Credits: Alamy Images: Jacques Jangoux 10tr; Corbis: Rick Doyle 16r; Ecoscene 24tr; Terry W. Eggers 29; Kevin Fleming 14tr; Nick Hawkes;
Jeremy Horner 10c; Alexandra E. Jones/Ecoscene 36tr; Sally A Morgan/Ecoscene 34tr; Paul Seheult/Eye Ubiquitous 22tr; Paul A. Souders 38r;
Nik Wheeler 26tr; Michael S. Yamashita 5; Getty Images: Steve Bronstein 17; Lester Lefkowitz 32tr; Holt Studios International: 1c;
Science Photo Library: 4b; Simon Fraser 12tr; George Post 28r; Tom van Sant/Geosphere Project/Planetary Visions 8cr. Jacket: Corbis/NASA t.

All other images: DK Dorling Kindersley © 2004. For further information see www.dkimages.com
Dorling Kindersley Ltd., 80 Strand, London WC2R ORL

Contents

The World Around You

Planet Earth consists of rock and metal. Water, air and soil are all interconnected with life on Earth. In this book there are experiments that explore water, air and soil. These experiments will help you understand how each resource is a partner with life on Earth. The experiments will also help you explore the natural cycles of these resources and how they change.

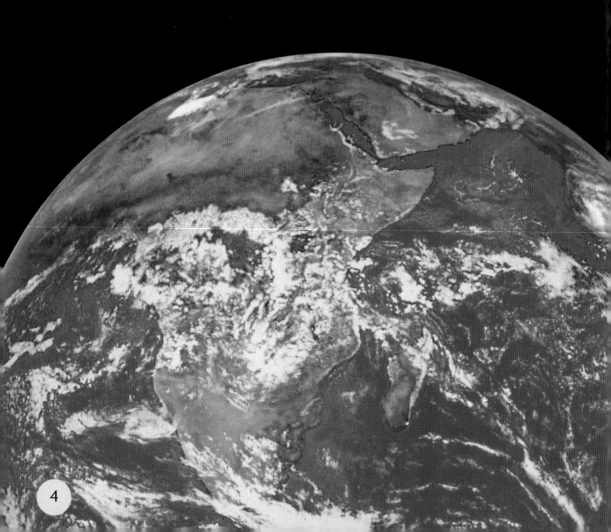

Exploring Water

Water is necessary for all life forms on Earth. In some areas there is too much water, and in others there is too little. However, throughout the Earth there is enough for everyone. Water never runs out because it is naturally recycled through the **water cycle**.

How Does the Water Cycle Work?

The **water cycle** starts over the oceans, seas and lakes. The water is heated by the Sun and evaporates, or rises as **water vapour**. Then, this vapour condenses and the tiny droplets form clouds which are blown by the wind. When the clouds become too heavy, the water returns to Earth as **precipitation** – rain, snow, sleet or hail. Some is absorbed by the soil and seeps into the rock layers below to form **groundwater**. Plant roots draw water from the soil and rocks, and plant leaves release water into the atmosphere. Precipitation also falls back directly into the oceans and other bodies of water. The water then evaporates again as the water cycle continues.

2. Water falls back to the Earth as rain, snow, sleet or hail.

1. Water evaporates from the Earth's surface.

3. Water flows back into the rivers and seas.

Purpose

The following experiment will show you how **evaporation** and condensation are parts of the water cycle. Follow the directions so you can see for yourself how these parts of the water cycle work.

Materials

- a small container
- a large plastic bowl
- water
- cling film
- an elastic band
- a weight, such as a small rock

Procedure

1 Place a small container in the middle of the base of a large bowl.

2 Pour water into the large bowl. The water level should go about halfway up the outside of the small container. (Do not get any water inside the small container.)

3 Cover the bowl tightly with cling film, using an elastic band to hold the cling film in place.

4 Place a small weight on top of and in the middle of the cling film "lid".

5 Put the bowl in the Sun and observe what happens.

? What Happens?

The Sun's heat turns the water into vapour, which rises to the cool plastic "lid" of the bowl. Here water droplets form. The weight causes a dip in the "lid" so that the water droplets roll towards the middle, merge and fall from the cling film into the small container.

How Can You Tell There is Water Vapour in the Air?

Nearly three-quarters of the Earth's surface is covered by water, but only about 24 per cent of all fresh water on Earth is available for us to use. On average, less than 1 per cent of this water is found in the air as **water vapour**. Yet all the world's **precipitation** comes from this small amount.

Most of the time, air looks and feels dry to us. However, it is never completely dry. Air always contains some water vapour through **evaporation**. We become more aware of water vapour when the air is humid.

This satellite photo of Earth taken above the Pacific Ocean shows us how much of Earth is covered with water.

Purpose

In the following experiment, you will see that there is always water vapour in the air, even though it is invisible to us and even when the air does not feel humid.

Materials

- a canned drink
- a fridge
- a saucer or a paper towel

Procedure

1 Place the canned drink in the fridge until the drink is very cold.

2 Remove the can from the fridge and place it on a saucer or paper towel.

3 Wait a few minutes and observe what happens.

? What Happens?

The can may appear to "sweat". Of course, it isn't sweating the way that people sweat. What is really happening? The water vapour in the room **condenses** on the cold can and forms droplets. This will occur only if the temperature of the can is lower than the current **dew point** temperature. This is the temperature that air must be cooled for dew, or condensation, to form. In a hot and dry climate this experiment may not produce any condensation.

How Can You Measure Rainfall?

In the experiment on pages 8 and 9, the **water vapour** droplets dripped down the side of the cold can. This is a model of how rain is formed. Raindrops are created by the condensation of water vapour into large droplets that fall back to the Earth.

Too little rain leads to droughts. Too much rain in too short a time leads to floods, which damage crops and property.

The Atacama Desert in Chile is the driest place in the world.

It rains on Mount Wai'ale'alei in Hawaii 350 days of the year.

Purpose

In the next experiment, you will make your own rain gauge. This is a tool used to collect and measure rainfall in an environment.

In the experiment on pages 8 and 9

Materials
- a clear plastic bottle
- scissors
- masking tape or duct tape
- a ruler
- marbles or pebbles
- water

Procedure

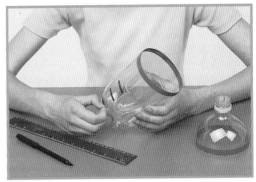

1 Ask an adult to cut off the top of a plastic bottle. The top part should have a narrow neck. The bottom part should be shaped like a cylinder. Cover the edges of both parts of the plastic bottle with tape.

2 Make measurement markers on the bottom part of the bottle. Place strips of tape at 2 cm intervals.

3 Put marbles or pebbles in the bottle. This will add stability. Now put the top of the bottle upside down, inside the cylindrical part of the bottle.

4 Fill the bottle with enough water to reach your first measurement line. This line, or strip of tape, is the zero mark, or baseline for measurement.

5 Put the rain gauge outside and find out how much rain falls over a period of time.

? What Happens?

The rain gauge allows rain to fall through the funnel into the container where it will not evaporate. As it rains, the water level rises. With the rain gauge, you can measure rainfall in one storm or over a period of time. Note: Use your rain gauge to test for **acid rain** (page 12), filter water (page 14) and test for air pollution in your neighbourhood (page 26).

How Can You Test the Acidity of Liquids?

Acid rain harms crops, makes animals sick and damages forests, lakes and buildings. Acid rain forms when **pollutants** from cars and factories are released into the air and mixed with **water vapour**. They form droplets of sulphuric and nitric acids which fall back to Earth in rainwater.

Even low levels of these acids are harmful. Too much nitrogen reduces the amount of oxygen in water. Aluminium from soils washed into lakes by acid rain poisons the fish. Since fish are eaten by other animals, acid rain upsets the ecological balance of an area. These same acids slowly eat statues and buildings away because the acids dissolve limestone, sandstone and marble.

Acid rain deprives tree roots and leaves of vital nutrients. Many trees eventually die.

Purpose

The following experiment will give you an opportunity to compare the acid in rain to the acid in other liquids. You can also determine which liquids would be helpful to our environment and which would be harmful.

Materials

- a rain gauge (see page 10)
- a rainwater sample
- an eyedropper
- a **pH** kit (available at pet shops)
- a notebook
- vinegar
- distilled water
- bicarbonate of soda solution (Mix 1 teaspoon of bicarbonate of soda in 115 ml of distilled water.)

Procedure

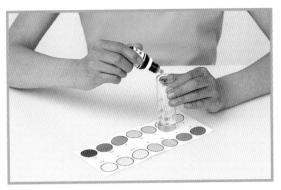

1 Collect rainwater in a rain gauge. Use an eyedropper to get a sample of rainwater.

2 Drop the rainwater sample onto the pH indicator in your pH kit. This will give you a measurement indicating the acidity level.

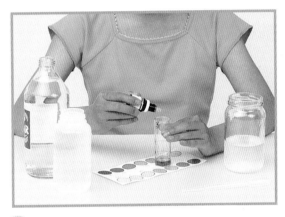

3 Record the pH level in your notebook, and discard the rainwater sample.

4 Wash out the eyedropper and pH indicator. Then repeat the same procedure with the vinegar, distilled water and bicarbonate of soda solution.

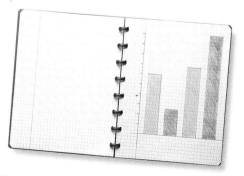

5 Record your findings in the notebook. Then plot a vertical graph to show the results.

? What Happens?

The indicator in the pH kit changes colour to show if the sample is acidic (below 7) or **alkaline** (above 7). **Precipitation** is considered harmful to fish and plants if its pH falls below 5.

How Can Water Be Cleaned?

Earth and its different environments have provided natural ways to keep water fresh and clean. For instance, sand beds naturally remove **pollutants** from **groundwater**, and waterways are cleaned by wetlands. However, with the increasing number of people and industries on Earth, other methods had to be invented to help nature to keep fresh water clean and drinkable.

Sewage is usually flushed away in water. Sewage treatment plants recycle this waste water. First dirty particles are screened out of the water. Then germ-killing chemicals and sometimes fluoride are added.

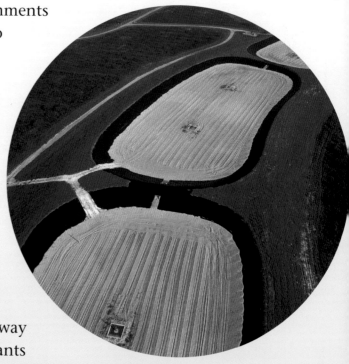

Sand beds filter out impurities in water.

Purpose

The following experiment will provide an example of how water can be filtered to make it clean. Note the many different types of filters used to catch different pollutants.

Materials

- a rain gauge (see page 10)
- coffee filter paper
- charcoal
- sand
- gravel
- a beaker
- dirty water (a mixture of tap water, potting soil, rice, flour, tea leaves and coffee grounds)

Procedure

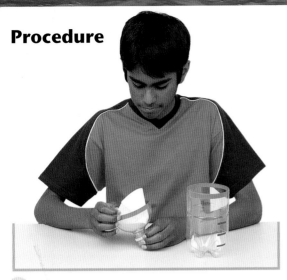

1 Use the rain gauge that you made in the experiment on page 10. Make sure that it is clean and empty. Line the top part of the rain gauge with the coffee filter paper.

2 Next put a layer of charcoal into the bottom of the lined neck, followed by a layer of sand, then a layer of gravel. Put the neck part back in the gauge.

Do not drink the filtered water. It will still have harmful substances and germs in it.

? What Happens?

As the dirty water seeps through the layers, different substances are filtered out. The gravel traps the biggest pieces and filter paper catches the smallest pieces.

3 Pour the dirty water into the rain gauge. After the water has drained through the filter into the bottom, pour it into an empty, clean beaker. What does it look like?

Conclusion

Water is maintained through the never-ending **water cycle**. The experiments in this section showed you the different aspects of the water cycle. You saw how water, or **precipitation**, falls to Earth and then is evaporated. You also saw how water **condenses**. You learned how to measure precipitation levels and now know how to test for **acid rain**. You also learned how to filter **pollutants** out of water. It is through experiments such as these that we learn about the water cycle.

Exploring Air

Air is all around us. It is made up of nitrogen, oxygen and small amounts of other gases. Air isn't generally seen, smelt or felt.

Earth is surrounded by a blanket of gases called the atmosphere. Oxygen is one of those gases. It is the most important gas for keeping us alive.

The atmosphere is held close to Earth by gravity. It extends to about 595 km from the Earth's surface and consists of four basic layers. In the higher layers the atmosphere becomes less dense and the air "thins out". It contains less oxygen and has lower **air pressure**.

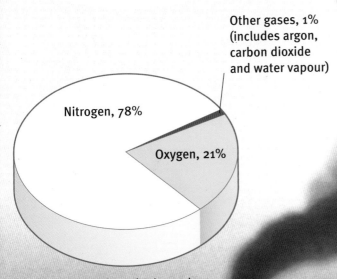

Other gases, 1%
(includes argon, carbon dioxide and water vapour)

Nitrogen, 78%

Oxygen, 21%

The air we breathe is made up of several gases.

How Does Air Pressure Change?

Air has weight. One litre of air weighs about as much as a small paper clip. The Earth's surface is at the bottom of the atmosphere. The weight of the atmosphere above pushes down on the Earth's surface. The higher you go in the sky, the lower the **air pressure**.

There are four basic layers that make up Earth's atmosphere. These layers are shown on the diagram. Weather is confined to the troposphere. In the stratosphere is the ozone layer. This filters out the Sun's harmful rays.

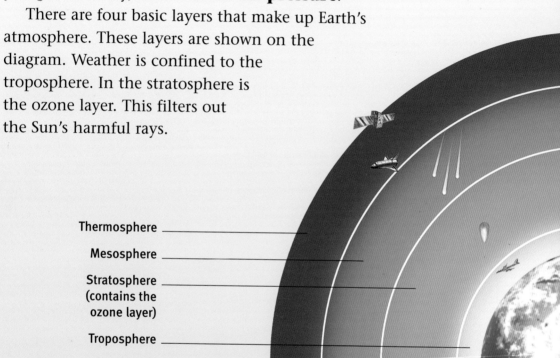

Thermosphere _____

Mesosphere _____

Stratosphere _____
(contains the
ozone layer)

Troposphere _____

Purpose

In the following experiment, you can see that air pressure decreases as you go higher into the atmosphere.

Materials

- cooking oil
- a large clear container
- plastic tubing or a straw
- tape

Procedure

1 Fill the container almost to the top with cooking oil.

2 Feed one end of the tube into the container so it nearly touches the bottom. Tape the tube to the rim of the container.

3 Blow gently into the other end of the tube.

? What Happens?

An air bubble emerges from the tube at the bottom of the container. It grows bigger as it rises up to the top of the container. Why? The air bubble is less dense than the oil, so the bubble rises. The pressure on the oil is lower at the top of the container than at the bottom. So as the air bubble rises, it expands.

How Can You Observe Air Pressure at Work?

Air pressure is affected by temperature. Since the Sun does not heat the atmosphere evenly, there are parts of the air that are warmer than other parts. When air becomes warmer, the air pressure decreases and the air rises. As air rises, it expands and cools.

Since cooler air cannot hold as much water as warmer air, the water **condenses** and forms clouds. So low pressure areas are often accompanied by rain. High pressure areas are made up of falling air. As the air falls, it becomes warmer and can hold more water. Areas of high pressure usually mean fair weather.

Weather maps show air pressure. Areas of high pressure are called highs (H). Areas of low pressure are called lows (L). Lines called isobars connect points of equal air pressure.

Areas of high and low air pressure are labelled on weather maps.

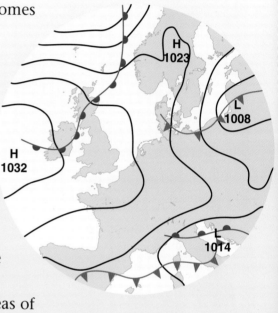

isobar	——
warm front	●●●
cold front	▲▲▲

Purpose

Weight is a real force. You can feel that force at work when a heavy book weighs down your hand. The amount of force exerted over a particular area is called pressure. The force of air pressure at work can be observed through the following experiment.

Materials

- a glass
- water
- a playing card

Procedure

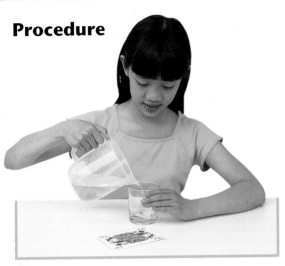

1 Fill the glass to the brim with water.

2 Wet the rim of the glass and carefully lay the card on top.

3 Firmly press one hand against the card and quickly turn the glass over. Take your hand away.

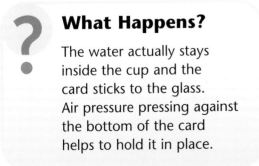

? What Happens?

The water actually stays inside the cup and the card sticks to the glass. Air pressure pressing against the bottom of the card helps to hold it in place.

How Can a Barometer Measure Air Pressure?

One way to predict the weather is to note changes in **air pressure**. **Meteorologists** measure air pressure with a **barometer**. A mercury barometer is a glass tube open at one end. The open end sits in mercury. Air pressure pushes the mercury up into the tube's vacuum. Another kind of barometer is a closed container with thin metal sides that bend with air pressure changes.

a barometer

Purpose

In 1643 Evangelista Torricelli invented the mercury barometer. His experiments showed how mercury levels in a tube could change with changes in air pressure. However, mercury is a dangerous poison that should not be handled. With the following experiment you can make a simple barometer that does not require mercury, and you can use it to record changes in air pressure.

Materials

- a glass
- a balloon
- an elastic band
- masking tape or duct tape
- a wooden board
- scissors
- a straw
- an index card
- a notebook
- a pencil

Procedure

1 Stretch the balloon over the top of the glass. Hold it in place with an elastic band.

2 Stick the glass to the wooden board to stop it from accidentally moving.

3 Cut one end of the straw to a point. Stick the uncut end onto the middle of the balloon that is attached to the glass. This will be your barometer pointer.

4 Make a measurement scale by placing marks 1 cm apart on the index card. Stick the card to the board so the pointer-end of the straw reaches the scale.

5 Record your observations in your notebook every day for a month. Include the number on the scale that the straw points to, the current weather and a comparison with the previous barometric measurement. If a storm is approaching, then you should record the level every fifteen to thirty minutes.

 What Happens?

The pointer rises as the air pressure outside the glass increases. It falls as air pressure drops. Why? The balloon changes shape (indenting inwards or bulging outwards) to keep the pressure inside the glass balanced with the pressure outside the glass.

How Does Air Move?

The Earth's atmosphere is nearly always moving. Some air movements are weak and end quickly. Others are strong and last a long time. Air moves in all directions. Wind has been described as "air in a hurry". Air that moves very quickly produces gales and hurricanes.

As warm air rises, **air pressure** is reduced. As cold air sinks, air pressure increases. When warm air rises, cold air moves into the space the warm air left behind.

Strong winds can bend tall trees.

Purpose

Water flows from a cold area of high pressure to a warm area of low pressure. This is basically the same way that air moves. This experiment will show you how water moves. This can serve as a good model for understanding how air, which we cannot see, also moves.

Materials

- 2 clear plastic bottles
- scissors
- tubing
- modelling clay
- 2 bowls
- hot water
- ice cubes
- 2 clips
- water to fill bottles
- red and blue food colouring
- sticky tape

Procedure

1 Ask an adult to cut the tops off the bottles and make two holes in each bottle. One hole should be 2 cm from the new top of the bottle and the other hole should be 2 cm from the bottom.

2 Cover the edges of the bottles with sticky tape. Cut two equal lengths of tubing and insert the ends into the holes to connect the two bottles. Seal the tubing into the holes using modelling clay.

3 Put one bottle in a bowl of hot water, the other in a bowl with ice. Clip the tubes and fill each bottle with water to cover the top tubing.

4 Add red food colouring to the bottle placed in warm water and blue food colouring to the bottle in ice. Remove the clips.

? What Happens?

The warm (red-coloured) water flows through the top tube. The cold (blue-coloured) water flows through the bottom tube. Why? The ice cubes cool the blue water, causing the pressure to rise. This increased pressure pushes down on the water, forcing it to flow out the bottom tube into the red, warm water. Meanwhile, the rising warmth draws the red water up, and it flows out the top tube into the bottle of cold water.

How Much Pollution is in the Air?

Air is filled with life-sustaining gases. Yet it has also become filled with a host of pollutants. Smoke and soot from factories, power plants and car exhausts pollute the air. Mixed together, these **pollutants** can produce smog. This is an unhealthy haze that hangs over large cities. Many countries have laws to help control or reduce air pollution. Some cars have anti-pollution devices. Some factories put filters on their chimneys to cut down on pollution.

Large cities are often blanketed with smog.

Purpose

In the following experiment, you can test the level of pollution in the air you breathe. If you live in a large city, then you have probably observed skies darkened by a blanket of smoke and fog. Smog contains fog and soot. If you have breathing problems, then smog might make you feel worse.

Materials

- a rain gauge (see page 10)
- a white coffee filter paper
- a magnifying glass

Procedure

1 Use the rain gauge you made for the experiment on page 10. Put filter paper into the neck part and place the rain gauge outside in a glass jar. Make sure the jar is secure.

2 Leave the rain gauge outside until it has filled with rainwater. Remove the filter paper and lay it flat on a table.

3 Examine your filter paper through a magnifying glass in good light.

? What Happens?

Particles in the air cling to the raindrops which fall through the air onto the filter paper. Dust, pollen, fungal spores and pollutants cling to the filter paper. If you see black specks then they may be particles of soot from fires or car exhausts.

Conclusion

Air plays a very important role in the lives of all living things. We all need air to live. For people with breathing problems or lung diseases, unhealthy air can be dangerous. For people who suffer from asthma, just getting enough air into the lungs can be a struggle.

Think about the different observations you made in the air experiments. You saw that air makes up the atmosphere. You explored how movement of air within the atmosphere changes weather conditions. By understanding more about air we can help to protect it.

Exploring Soil

Soil is a mixture of decaying plants and animals and small pieces of rock from the bedrock below. Nutrients in the decaying material and the minerals in the broken down rocks make soil a good home for plants, insects and other small animals. There are also many tiny gaps within the soil. These gaps are filled with air and water. Each of these resources helps to break down further rock pieces into finer grains, improve the quality of the soil and speed up the process of decay.

How Do You Measure Air in Soil?

Rocks break down over time. They are worn away in a process called weathering. Changes in temperature, melting or freezing water, and the root actions of trees are all types of weathering. So are certain chemical processes that can break rocks apart, turning them into soil filled with pockets of air and water.

Plant roots break rock into smaller pieces while searching for water and nutrients.

Purpose

In the following experiment, you can test your own samples and measure the amount of air space a soil sample contains. Knowing this information can help you identify the soil's texture. Knowing a soil's texture helps to determine what types of plants can be grown in it.

Materials
- soil samples, taken from your garden
- 2 large measuring jugs
- a trowel
- water
- a bucket

Procedure

1 Use the trowel to put the soil in a measuring jug. Make sure the soil is level. Read and record the quantity in the jug.

2 Measure out an identical quantity of water. Pour the water into the measuring jug filled with soil.

3 Read and record the new level. To work out the air space, add the quantity of the original soil sample and the quantity of the water. Subtract the quantity of the final product from this sum. This figure represents the amount of air space in the original soil sample.

What Happens?

Water fills in some of the air gaps in the soil, so the combined level is less than the sum of the original soil level and the original water level. A fine-textured soil has smaller particles, but more spaces to hold air and water than a coarse soil which contains larger particles. Therefore, fine soil can hold more water than coarse soil.

What Else is in Soil?

Sometimes soil is carried away from where it formed by running water, glaciers, wind or waves. It is then moved to a new place where it may have a different chemical make-up from the new bedrock below it. In time, the make-up of the soil will also be changed by the type of plants that grow on it and by weather conditions. Plants may use up the minerals in the soil, or water may wash away minerals completely.

On farms, minerals are replaced before new crops are planted. Farmers add fertilisers to soil to replace missing minerals.

Purpose

Soils can be made up of different-size grains and contain organic matter, such as leaves and twigs. In this experiment, you can see what is in your soil sample and its basic grain size, or texture.

Materials

- a soil sample
- weighing scales
- a newspaper
- a magnifying glass
- tweezers
- 5 jars
- labels
- a pen
- a trowel
- a coarse-mesh sieve
- a fine-mesh sieve

Procedure

1 Weigh the soil sample and spread it out on newspaper. Use tweezers to pick out organic material. Store live animals in one jar. Put the other organic material in a separate jar.

2 Move the soil sample into the coarse-mesh sieve and shake it. Weigh the coarse material that is left in the sieve. Store this portion of the soil in a labelled jar.

3 Move the rest of the soil into the fine-mesh sieve and shake it. Weigh the medium-grained material that is left in the sieve and the fine-grained material that went through. Store these portions of the soil in two separate labelled jars.

? What Happens?

Live organisms, other organic material, coarse material (such as stones and large particles), medium-grained material and fine-grained material make up the soil sample. Note the proportions of each type of material in your soil sample. Try the experiment with other samples such as potting soil or soil from another area. How are they different?

How Acidic is Soil?

The acidity of soil varies from place to place. Most plants grow well in slightly acidic soil. If a soil is rich in organic materials, such as decaying roots and leaves, the soil probably has a high acid content. Soil may contain too much acid if the rainwater in the area is very acidic. A soil can be made more acidic by adding peat moss or sulphur. Ground limestone can be added to make it less acidic.

This forest floor is covered in organic matter, making the soil acidic.

Purpose

Chemists measure the acidity of soils using the **pH** scale. In the following experiment, you will test soil acidity levels. The lower the number below 7, the greater the acid content of the soil.

Materials

- a knife
- a chopping board
- red cabbage
- a pot
- purified water
- a sieve
- a jug
- 5 jars
- labels
- a pen
- 4 soil samples (peat moss, sand, potting soil, fertiliser)
- hydrated or powdered lime (found in garden centres)

Procedure

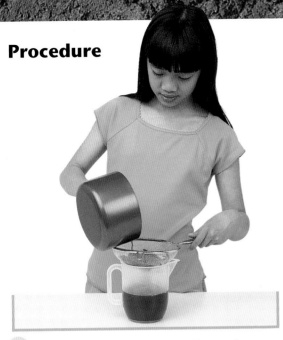

1 Ask an adult to cut up half a red cabbage and heat 1 litre of purified water in a pot. Add the chopped cabbage to the heated water, and let it sit for 30 minutes. Then use the sieve to strain the liquid into a jug.

2 Add a little red cabbage water to each of the four soil samples which have been placed in labelled jars. Pour the remaining cabbage water into a labelled jar.

Wash your hands after adding the powdered lime.

3 Add lime to the soil sample with the reddest water, and observe what happens.

? What Happens?

Acidic soil turns the cabbage water redder. The more acid the soil contains, the redder the cabbage water gets. Soil that is not acidic is **alkaline**. Alkaline soil turns the cabbage water blue. The more alkaline it is, the bluer the cabbage water gets. Adding lime neutralises the acid level and causes the cabbage water to turn bluish in colour.

What Causes Soil Erosion?

Soil **erosion** is caused by wind, flooding, overgrazing or mismanagement. It can ruin in a few years soil that has taken tens of thousands of years to create. It is a serious problem in very dry, windy places such as northern Africa. It is also a growing problem in tropical rainforests. Millions of hectares of rainforest are cleared each year for farmland or pastures. After a few seasons, this soil has no nutrients and is no longer fertile. New parts of the rainforest are then cleared to replace the "used up" land. As this cycle continues, more and more of the once-lush rainforest loses vegetation.

This patch of land is suffering from deforestation.

Purpose

One way to stop running water from eroding soil is to plant grass that absorbs the water. Rows of trees can also act as windbreaks to stop soil from blowing away. In the following experiment, you can see the effect on soil if no vegetation is present.

Materials

- 2 shallow baking trays
- sticks, leaves and small rocks
- soil
- 2 plastic tubs
- a timer or stopwatch
- building blocks
- a watering can
- a rain gauge (see page 11)
- a coffee filter
- 2 jars

Procedure

1 Spread equal amounts of soil on the two trays. Then sprinkle a handful of leaves, sticks and rocks over the soil in one tray.

2 Use the blocks to prop up one end of both trays so they tilt at the same angle. Then place the plastic tubs below the trays to catch the water that runs off.

3 Slowly pour the same amount of water over each tray. Start the timer or stopwatch as the water run-off begins. Measure the amount of time it takes for all the water to run down into each tub.

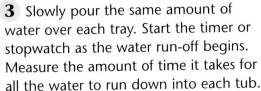

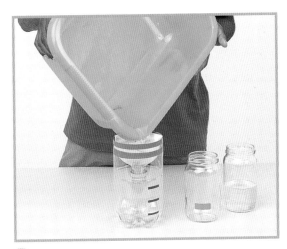

4 Filter the water in each tub by pouring it through a coffee filter in the rain gauge. Pour the filtered water into two jars and compare.

? What Happens?

The plain soil is quickly washed away, and the water is much dirtier. The plant debris slows the erosion. It also filters the water.

Conclusion

Soil contains water and air as well as the Earth's weathered rocks and decaying organic matter. Through the experiments in this book you have been shown how to work out the composition and texture of soil and how to evaluate the acid level in soil. You have also been shown how loss of vegetation contributes to soil **erosion**.

Water, air and soil are all valuable resources that need to be protected and conserved. Through these experiments, you have seen how each of these resources can affect the Earth and the environment where you live. Why not continue to experiment and explore the world around you and look for even more ways to help preserve our resources?

Glossary

acid rain   rain that forms when air pollutants from cars and factories mix with water vapour and fall back to Earth as rainwater

air pressure   the pressure exerted by the Earth's atmosphere at any given point

alkaline   having a pH greater than 7

barometer   a device that measures pressure in the atmosphere

condenses   changes from a gas or vapour to a liquid or solid form

dew point   the temperature to which air must be cooled for moisture to form

erosion   the process by which the surface of the Earth is worn away by water, glaciers, winds and waves

evaporation   the process of turning water from a liquid into a gas

groundwater   water in the ground near the Earth's surface

meteorologist   a scientist who studies the atmosphere including weather and climate

pH   measure of the level of acidity in a substance

pollutants   harmful substances in the environment

precipitation   rain, snow, sleet or hail

water cycle   a continuous cycle in which water on Earth evaporates, rises as vapour to form clouds and falls back to Earth again as precipitation

water vapour   gasey water below its boiling point

Index